The New Rich

The New Rich

Matthew Petchinsky

1

The New Rich: How to Retire by 35

By: Matthew Petchinsky

Disclaimer

This book, *The New Rich: How to Retire by 35*, is intended for **educational and informational purposes only**. It is not financial, legal, tax, investment, or professional advice of any kind. The strategies, concepts, frameworks, examples, and philosophies presented within these pages are based on general principles, personal insights, and hypothetical scenarios designed to encourage critical thinking, self-reflection, and long-term planning—not to serve as individualized financial guidance.

Nothing in this book should be interpreted as a promise, guarantee, or assurance of financial success, wealth, income, or early retirement. Individual results will vary significantly depending on personal circumstances, effort, discipline, economic conditions, geographic location, risk tolerance, health, education, and many other factors beyond the author's control. Any references to income, lifestyle outcomes, or timelines are illustrative only and should not be considered typical or expected results.

The author is not a licensed financial advisor, investment advisor, tax professional, attorney, or accountant. Readers are strongly encouraged to consult qualified professionals before making financial, legal, tax, or investment decisions. Any actions taken based on the information in this book are done at the reader's own discretion and risk.

This book may discuss concepts such as entrepreneurship, digital income, automation, investing, content creation, or alternative income models. These topics inherently involve uncertainty and risk, including the potential for financial loss. The author expressly disclaims any liability for financial losses, emotional distress, business failure, or life disruptions that may occur as a result of applying or misapplying the ideas presented.

References to wealth, success, freedom, or "retirement" are philosophical and strategic in nature. "Retiring by 35" does not necessarily imply permanent cessation of work or guaranteed financial independence, but rather the ability to design one's life with greater autonomy, flexibility, and intentionality. Definitions of success vary from person to person, and readers are encouraged to define success in ways that align with their own values, health, responsibilities, and circumstances.

Any examples, stories, or scenarios used in this book are illustrative and may be fictionalized or generalized to protect privacy and enhance learning. They are not representations of specific individuals unless explicitly stated.

This book does not replace personal responsibility, professional advice, or due diligence. Readers assume full responsibility for their decisions, actions, and outcomes after engaging with the material.

By reading this book, you acknowledge and agree that the author and publisher are not liable for any decisions you make or results you experience as a result of the information provided.

Introduction: Redefining Wealth and Retirement

For generations, wealth has been defined narrowly—measured in bank balances, job titles, square footage, and the number of years a person can endure work before finally being "allowed" to rest. Retirement, in this outdated model, is not freedom but a delayed reward: something granted only after decades of exhaustion, compliance, and postponement of life itself.

This book challenges that entire narrative.

The New Rich is not about becoming wealthy in the traditional sense. It is about reclaiming ownership over your time, your energy, your attention, and your future—long before the conventional finish line. It is about redefining what it means to live well, to work with intention, and to design a life that supports your humanity rather than consumes it.

Retiring by 35 is not a fantasy, nor is it a guarantee. It is a framework. A mindset shift. A strategic reimagining of how money, labor, creativity, and autonomy interact in a world that no longer rewards loyalty the way it once promised to.

The Old Model Is Breaking

The traditional model of success was built for a world that no longer exists. It assumed stable employment, predictable pensions, rising wages, and a linear career path. Today's reality is different. Jobs disappear overnight. Skills become obsolete in years, sometimes months. Economic shocks ripple globally. Burnout is normalized. Time is traded for money until health, curiosity, and joy quietly erode.

Many people feel this instinctively. They sense that something is wrong, but they're told the solution is simply to work harder, hustle longer, or wait patiently for a future that keeps moving further away.

This book exists because that advice no longer works.

Wealth as Autonomy, Not Excess

In this framework, wealth is not defined by luxury or status. It is defined by **optionality**—the ability to choose how your days unfold. True wealth is waking up without panic, without dread, without the feeling that your life belongs to someone else.

Wealth is having:

- Control over your time
- Flexibility in your income
- Emotional and mental space to think clearly
- The ability to say no without fear
- The freedom to pivot when life changes

This book does not ask you to abandon ambition. It asks you to redirect it—away from endless accumulation and toward sustainable independence.

Retirement Reimagined

Retirement, as used in this book, does not mean stopping all work or withdrawing from the world. It means **retiring from dependency**, from urgency, from survival mode. It means building systems that support you rather than drain you.

You may still work. You may still create. You may even earn more than ever before. But you are no longer trapped by the necessity of constant output just to remain afloat.

In this sense, retirement becomes a state of leverage, not an age.

A New Kind of Strategy

This book does not offer get-rich-quick schemes, shortcuts, or promises of effortless wealth. Instead, it presents a framework for building financial resilience through clarity, focus, and intelligent leverage.

You will explore:

- How modern wealth is built quietly, not loudly
- Why attention is the most valuable currency of the digital age
- How small, repeatable systems outperform burnout-driven ambition
- Why sustainable income beats explosive success
- How identity, psychology, and belief quietly shape financial outcomes

The goal is not perfection. The goal is momentum—designed on your terms.

You Are Not Late

One of the most damaging myths of modern culture is that if you haven't "made it" by a certain age, you've failed. This book rejects that lie completely. There is no universal timeline. There is only alignment.

Many of the most impactful transformations occur not when everything is in place—but when clarity finally arrives. This book meets you wherever you are and treats that point as valid, workable, and full of possibility.

This Is a Blueprint, Not a Promise

What follows is not a formula to copy blindly, but a framework to adapt. You are encouraged to question, adjust, and personalize everything you read. The goal is not imitation—it is self-authorship.

By the end of this book, you may not have retired. But you will understand how to build toward freedom deliberately, ethically, and sustainably. You will understand what kind of "rich" actually matters to you—and how to stop chasing versions of success that were never yours to begin with.

This is not about escaping life.

It is about finally living it—on your terms.

Chapter 1: The Death of Traditional Retirement Plans

The Illusion of Security

For decades, society sold a single story about safety: work hard, stay loyal, climb slowly, and one day you will be rewarded with rest. This promise was repeated so often it became cultural truth. Retirement was portrayed as a finish line—something guaranteed if you followed the rules, showed up on time, and didn't ask too many questions. Entire generations organized their lives around this belief, trusting institutions to protect their future.

But that version of security was never permanent. It relied on economic conditions that no longer exist: stable pensions, affordable housing, predictable inflation, and long-term employer loyalty. Over time, those pillars eroded quietly while the narrative stayed the same. The rules changed, but the instructions never did.

Today, many people discover too late that their "retirement plan" was built on assumptions that no longer hold. Pensions disappear. Social systems strain. Healthcare costs explode. Inflation eats savings silently. What was once a promise becomes a gamble—and often, a losing one.

This chapter is not about blame. It is about clarity. The traditional retirement model didn't fail because people were lazy or careless. It failed because the world evolved faster than the systems designed to support it.

Recognizing this is not pessimism—it is empowerment. You cannot fix what you do not see clearly.

Why the Old Path No Longer Works

The traditional retirement model assumes linear progress: steady income, predictable raises, long-term employment, and a clean exit at a predetermined age. But modern life is nonlinear. Careers fracture. Industries collapse. Technology reshapes entire professions overnight.

Many people now change careers multiple times, not by choice but by necessity. Gig work replaces stability. Benefits shrink. Lifelong employment becomes a myth told by previous generations who lived under vastly different economic conditions.

The old system also assumes energy is infinite. It presumes you can push relentlessly in your youth and simply "rest later." In reality, burnout accumulates. Chronic stress compounds. Health issues appear earlier. Emotional exhaustion sets in long before financial freedom does.

Traditional retirement planning also disconnects money from meaning. It treats life as something to endure before enjoyment is allowed. This creates a quiet despair—people surviving instead of living, waiting for permission to be free.

The system isn't broken because people failed. It's broken because it was never designed for the world we live in now.

The Hidden Cost of Waiting

Waiting has a cost that rarely appears on spreadsheets. Every year spent postponing freedom trains the nervous system to accept confinement. Over time, people stop dreaming, stop experimenting, and stop believing that change is possible.

Deferred living creates emotional debt. Resentment builds quietly. Creativity atrophies. People begin to equate safety with stagnation and mistake exhaustion for responsibility.

This cost is rarely discussed because it is difficult to measure. But it shows up in anxiety, irritability, disengagement, and the haunting sense that life is happening somewhere else.

When people finally reach the age they were told would bring freedom, many discover they no longer have the energy—or the identity—to enjoy it. They spent decades preparing for a future self they barely recognize.

This is not a personal failure. It is a design flaw.

Redefining What "Retirement" Really Means

Retirement, as reframed in this book, is not an age or an event. It is a condition of autonomy. It is the ability to choose how you spend your time without fear of collapse.

This version of retirement is fluid. It can exist in stages. It can coexist with work, creation, and contribution. It does not require waiting until your body is tired or your curiosity is gone.

Instead of asking, "When can I stop working?" the better question becomes, "How can I stop being trapped?"

This shift changes everything. It opens the door to designing systems that support your life now—not decades from now. It allows for progress without postponement.

Freedom is no longer a destination. It becomes a direction.

The Psychological Shift That Changes Everything

The greatest obstacle to financial freedom is not a lack of money—it is the internalized belief that suffering is required. Many people unconsciously equate worth with struggle. If something feels easier, they assume it must be wrong.

This mindset keeps people tethered to outdated systems long after those systems stop serving them. It creates guilt around rest and suspicion toward ease.

Breaking this pattern requires unlearning. It requires recognizing that stability does not have to be earned through exhaustion. That security can be built through alignment, strategy, and adaptability rather than sacrifice alone.

Once this shift occurs, new options become visible. Possibilities that once seemed unrealistic begin to feel practical. Not because the world suddenly changed—but because perception did.

Mindset Shift 1: From "Someday" to "Now"

The traditional retirement narrative trains people to delay life. Joy becomes conditional. Freedom becomes hypothetical. This mindset quietly steals decades of presence.

Reframing begins by recognizing that waiting is often a habit, not a necessity. Many people delay action not because they lack resources, but because they were taught that action must wait for permission, stability, or perfection.

Choosing "now" does not mean recklessness. It means building with intention today instead of postponing alignment until some imaginary future. Small, deliberate steps compound faster than grand plans delayed indefinitely.

When "now" becomes your starting point, momentum replaces fear. You stop preparing to live and start living with awareness.

Mindset Shift 2: From Security to Adaptability

Traditional security is static. It assumes the world will stay predictable. Adaptability, on the other hand, thrives in change.

Financial resilience today comes from flexibility—diverse skills, multiple income channels, and the ability to learn quickly. This form of security moves with you instead of anchoring you to a single outcome.

Adaptability transforms uncertainty from a threat into a tool. When you can pivot, experiment, and recover, risk becomes manageable rather than paralyzing.

This mindset doesn't eliminate fear—it teaches you how to move with it.

Mindset Shift 3: From Accumulation to Alignment

Accumulation focuses on more: more money, more status, more proof. Alignment focuses on fit—how your work, values, and life actually feel together.

Aligned wealth supports your health, relationships, and time. It doesn't demand that you sacrifice one area of life to maintain another.

When alignment becomes the metric, success stops being external validation and starts becoming internal coherence. You measure progress by peace, agency, and sustainability—not by comparison.

This shift is subtle, but it changes everything.

Journal Prompts

1. What did I believe retirement would look like when I was younger, and where did that belief come from?
2. In what ways has waiting for "someday" limited my current life?
3. What does freedom actually mean to me—emotionally, not financially?
4. Which parts of my life feel most constrained right now?
5. What fears arise when I imagine redefining success on my own terms?
6. Where have I mistaken endurance for strength?
7. What systems in my life support me—and which drain me?
8. How do I personally define security, separate from society's definition?
9. What would a small step toward autonomy look like this month?
10. If I could design my life without fear of judgment, what would change first?

Closing Reflection

The collapse of the traditional retirement model is not a crisis—it is an invitation. An invitation to question inherited beliefs, to release outdated expectations, and to build something more humane and responsive to the reality of modern life.

You are not behind. You are early in a new era of thinking.

As you move forward, remember: freedom is not a finish line you cross one day. It is a practice you cultivate through awareness, intention, and choice.

The old map no longer leads where you want to go.

It's time to draw a new one.

Chapter 2: Digital Assets and Passive Income Streams

The Shift from Labor to Leverage

For most of modern history, income was tied directly to presence. You worked, you were paid. You stopped working, the money stopped too. This arrangement shaped how people understood value, effort, and worth. Labor became synonymous with survival, and time became something to sell in pieces.

Digital assets quietly disrupted this equation. They introduced the possibility that work could be done once and paid repeatedly. Not through exploitation or shortcuts, but through leverage—systems that continue producing value after the initial effort is complete.

This shift is subtle but revolutionary. It transforms labor from an ongoing transaction into an upfront investment. Instead of constantly trading hours for income, you build structures that operate independently of your daily presence.

This does not eliminate effort. It repositions it. Energy is front-loaded rather than endlessly drained. Creativity becomes infrastructure. Thought becomes capital.

Understanding this shift is foundational to redefining wealth in the modern world.

What Digital Assets Really Are

A digital asset is not just a file or a product. It is a container for value that can be distributed, duplicated, and accessed without your physical involvement. It may be a book, a course, a system, a framework, a template, or a body of knowledge shaped into a usable form.

What makes digital assets powerful is not their format, but their scalability. One hour of focused creation can reach hundreds, thousands, or millions of people without requiring proportional effort each time.

This scalability changes the relationship between time and income. Instead of trading more hours for more money, you expand reach. Instead of exhaustion, you focus on refinement.

Digital assets also allow you to work asynchronously. You create once, and the value travels forward—across time zones, schedules, and circumstances—without your presence.

This is the foundation of passive income, not as a myth, but as a system.

Passive Income Is Built, Not Discovered

Passive income is often misunderstood as effortless income. In reality, it is deferred effort. The work is done upfront so that future income requires less active input.

Most people fail here because they expect immediate results or underestimate the importance of quality. Passive income does not reward speed—it rewards clarity, usefulness, and consistency.

Successful digital assets solve real problems, answer real questions, or fulfill genuine needs. They create trust. Over time, that trust compounds into reliability.

The truth is uncomfortable but empowering: passive income is rarely passive in the beginning. It is intentional, strategic, and often quiet work that compounds invisibly before it becomes visible.

Those who understand this stop chasing shortcuts and start building systems.

Ownership Changes Everything

When you own a digital asset, you own leverage. You are no longer dependent on permission, schedules, or gatekeepers to earn. Ownership introduces autonomy into the economic equation.

This is why digital assets are so transformative. They convert effort into equity. They turn creativity into infrastructure. They allow individuals to operate with the leverage once reserved for institutions.

Ownership also changes mindset. You begin thinking in systems rather than tasks, longevity rather than urgency. You ask not, "How can I make money today?" but "What can I build that serves people for years?"

This shift marks the beginning of true financial independence.

Sustainability Over Scale

Many people pursue scale before stability. They chase virality, growth hacks, and rapid expansion without grounding their systems. This often leads to burnout or collapse.

Sustainable income is built through alignment. The work must fit your capacity, your values, and your life rhythms. Otherwise, the system will eventually reject you.

Digital assets thrive when they are maintainable. When creation does not require constant stress. When updates are manageable. When growth feels supportive rather than extractive.

Sustainability ensures that your income supports your life—not the other way around.

Mindset Shift 1: From Effort to Leverage

Most people equate value with effort. If something feels hard, it must be worthwhile. This belief keeps people stuck in cycles of overwork.

Leverage reframes effort as design. You invest energy once to create ongoing returns. This does not diminish the value of work—it refines it.

When you prioritize leverage, you stop asking how hard you can work and start asking how intelligently you can structure your output.

Mindset Shift 2: From Consumption to Creation

Modern culture trains people to consume endlessly. Scroll, watch, buy, repeat. Creation disrupts this pattern.

When you shift from consumption to creation, your relationship with content changes. You stop being passive and start becoming intentional.

This mindset transforms how you see time, ideas, and opportunity. You become a contributor rather than a spectator.

Mindset Shift 3: From Scarcity to Systems

Scarcity thinking focuses on lack—lack of time, money, energy. Systems thinking focuses on flow.

When you build systems, you reduce dependence on motivation and willpower. You allow structure to carry you forward.

This shift creates stability. Instead of chasing income, you design environments where income emerges naturally.

Journal Prompts

1. What skills or knowledge do I already have that could be turned into a digital asset?
2. Where am I still trading time for money out of habit rather than necessity?
3. What kind of work energizes me enough to sustain long-term creation?
4. How do I currently define passive income, and where did that belief come from?
5. What would a sustainable income system look like for my lifestyle?
6. Where do I feel resistance around ownership or visibility?
7. What systems in my life already work well that I could expand?
8. What fears arise when I imagine income not tied to constant effort?
9. How could I simplify my approach to earning?
10. What is one small digital asset I could begin building this month?

Closing Reflection

Digital assets are not about escaping work—they are about redefining it. They allow your effort to echo beyond the moment it is created. They turn intention into structure and creativity into continuity.

When you build assets instead of chasing paychecks, you begin to reclaim your time, your energy, and your sense of agency. You stop reacting to life and start designing it.

This chapter marks a turning point. You are no longer preparing to work harder—you are learning how to work wiser.

What you build next will not just earn for you.

It will support the life you are becoming.

Chapter 3: Minimalism and Wealth — Why Less Is More

The Illusion of More

Modern culture teaches a subtle but powerful equation: more possessions equal more success, more comfort, more happiness. From an early age, we are trained to measure progress through accumulation—bigger homes, newer technology, fuller calendars, busier lives. The message is constant and reinforced everywhere: more is better.

Yet for many, the pursuit of "more" quietly becomes a trap. More expenses. More obligations. More stress. More mental clutter. The very things meant to signal success begin to consume the freedom they were supposed to provide.

Minimalism challenges this assumption at its core. It asks a radical question: *What if less is not a sacrifice, but an upgrade?*

This chapter explores how intentional simplicity creates financial power, emotional clarity, and strategic freedom. Not by deprivation—but by design.

The Hidden Cost of Excess

Every possession carries a hidden price. Not just in money, but in attention, maintenance, decision-making, and emotional energy. Clutter is not neutral—it drains cognitive bandwidth and quietly taxes your focus.

Excess creates noise. It fragments attention and reduces the mental space needed for creativity, strategic thinking, and peace. When your environment is crowded, your mind follows.

Financial stress often isn't caused by lack of income alone, but by complexity. Multiple subscriptions, unused purchases, and lifestyle inflation quietly siphon resources without providing proportional value.

Minimalism exposes these leaks. It doesn't demand asceticism—it invites discernment.

Minimalism as a Wealth Strategy

True minimalism is not about having nothing. It's about keeping what serves you and releasing what doesn't. This distinction is critical.

When spending aligns with values, money becomes a tool instead of a trap. You stop buying to impress, distract, or numb. Instead, you invest in things that multiply freedom—time, health, knowledge, flexibility.

Minimalism increases your financial runway. Fewer obligations mean lower required income. Lower required income creates choice. Choice creates power.

This is why minimalism is not about deprivation—it is about leverage.

The Psychological Freedom of Less

There is a profound mental shift that occurs when you stop measuring worth by accumulation. You begin to feel lighter, clearer, and more intentional. Decisions become easier. Distractions lose their pull.

Minimalism removes the constant background noise of comparison. When you stop chasing someone else's version of success, you regain your own rhythm.

This psychological space is fertile ground for creativity and focus. With fewer distractions, you begin to notice what actually matters. You make choices from clarity instead of pressure.

This internal quiet is one of the most underrated forms of wealth.

Minimalism as a Foundation for Passive Income

Minimalism and passive income reinforce each other. When your lifestyle costs are intentionally low, your income goals become realistic and reachable.

You don't need millions to feel secure if your needs are modest and your systems are efficient. This allows you to build digital assets without desperation or burnout.

Minimalism also improves execution. Fewer commitments mean more energy to refine, optimize, and grow what truly matters. It encourages focus over fragmentation.

This synergy—low overhead and high leverage—is where sustainable freedom emerges.

Mindset Shift 1: From Accumulation to Alignment

Accumulation asks, "What can I add?"
Alignment asks, "What actually belongs?"

This shift changes consumption from impulse to intention. You stop chasing upgrades and start curating a life that reflects your values.

When your environment aligns with who you are becoming, progress feels natural rather than forced.

Mindset Shift 2: From Ownership to Stewardship

Ownership often implies control. Stewardship implies responsibility and care.

When you see your possessions as tools rather than trophies, you use them more wisely. You stop hoarding and start optimizing.

This mindset encourages sustainability—not just financially, but emotionally and environmentally.

Mindset Shift 3: From Busyness to Presence

Busyness is often mistaken for productivity. In reality, it frequently masks avoidance or insecurity.

Minimalism creates space for presence. When life is less crowded, attention sharpens. You become more intentional with your time, energy, and relationships.

Presence is where fulfillment lives—and it requires room to breathe.

Journal Prompts

1. What possessions in my life add stress rather than value?
2. Where am I confusing comfort with clutter?
3. How would my finances change if my needs were simpler?
4. What does "enough" mean to me personally?
5. Which expenses no longer align with my values?
6. How does my environment affect my mental clarity?
7. What am I holding onto out of habit rather than purpose?
8. What would my ideal, simplified day look like?
9. How might less responsibility create more freedom?
10. What would I gain by letting go?

Closing Reflection

Minimalism is not about having less—it's about having *space*. Space to think, to choose, to create, and to rest without guilt.

When you remove excess, you uncover clarity. When you reduce noise, you amplify meaning. And when you stop chasing more, you often find you already have enough.

Wealth is not measured by accumulation alone. It is measured by ease, autonomy, and peace.

By choosing less with intention, you make room for what truly matters—and that is where real wealth begins.

Chapter 4: How to Create a Life Where Work Is Optional

Redefining the Role of Work

For most people, work is positioned as a requirement for survival rather than a choice. From a young age, we're taught that labor equals worth, productivity equals value, and rest must be earned. This conditioning becomes so embedded that imagining a life where work is optional feels irresponsible—or even dangerous.

But optional work does not mean uselessness or idleness. It means **choice**. It means that work becomes something you *opt into* rather than something you are trapped inside. It means your life does not collapse if you stop producing for a period of time.

Creating a life where work is optional requires a fundamental shift in how work is defined. Work becomes an expression of purpose, curiosity, or service—not a survival mechanism. This reframing allows you to engage with work from a place of autonomy rather than obligation.

Optional work is not about laziness. It is about sovereignty.

Decoupling Survival from Labor

The most radical aspect of financial freedom is separating your basic needs from your daily labor. When survival depends on constant output, fear becomes the primary motivator. Fear narrows thinking, discourages risk, and traps people in cycles of compliance.

To make work optional, survival must be stabilized independently. This doesn't require wealth—it requires structure. Predictable expenses, controlled liabilities, and reliable income streams create a foundation that reduces urgency.

When your basic needs are met without constant effort, your nervous system settles. You gain clarity. Decision-making improves. Creativity returns.

This is not about escaping responsibility—it's about creating breathing room.

Designing Income That Serves You

Optional work is supported by income that doesn't demand constant attention. This includes digital assets, automated systems, royalties, licensing, and repeatable services that don't rely on hourly input.

The key is not volume, but consistency. A modest, reliable income stream that covers essentials is more powerful than an unstable high-income role that drains energy.

Designing this kind of income requires patience. Systems must be built, tested, refined, and allowed to mature. But once in place, they provide resilience—income that continues even during rest, illness, or transition.

This is the quiet power of leverage.

Time as the Ultimate Currency

When work becomes optional, time regains its true value. You are no longer trading hours for survival, but choosing how to invest them.

Time becomes a tool for creativity, learning, relationships, and restoration. You can pursue interests without monetizing them. You can rest without guilt. You can say no without fear.

This shift reorients life around presence rather than pressure. Days become intentional rather than reactive.

Wealth, in this sense, is not measured in money—but in moments you fully own.

Designing a Life, Not Escaping One

Many people dream of escape: quitting jobs, quitting cities, quitting systems. But escape without intention often recreates the same pressures in a new form.

Design is different. Design is deliberate. It asks: What kind of days do I want? What level of responsibility feels sustainable? What kind of work energizes rather than drains?

When you design your life, work becomes one component among many—not the axis everything else revolves around.

This approach creates resilience. Even when circumstances change, the underlying structure supports adaptation rather than collapse.

Mindset Shift 1: From Dependence to Autonomy

Dependence trains you to wait for permission. Autonomy teaches you to assess and decide.

This shift doesn't mean rejecting collaboration or support—it means refusing to surrender agency. You move from reacting to circumstances to shaping them.

Autonomy builds confidence. It creates internal stability that no external change can fully disrupt.

Mindset Shift 2: From Productivity to Sustainability

Productivity measures output. Sustainability measures longevity.

When you prioritize sustainability, you stop asking, “How much can I do?” and start asking, “How long can I do this without harm?”

This mindset protects energy, health, and creativity. It allows growth without burnout.

Mindset Shift 3: From Escape to Intentional Living

Escapism seeks relief. Intentional living builds alignment.

Instead of running from dissatisfaction, you begin designing environments and systems that support who you are becoming.

Work becomes optional not because you flee it, but because your life no longer depends on it.

Journal Prompts

1. What does "optional work" mean to me personally?
2. Which parts of my current work feel draining versus energizing?
3. What would I do differently if my basic needs were already covered?
4. Where am I overworking out of fear rather than necessity?
5. What systems could reduce my dependence on constant labor?
6. How does my body respond to my current work rhythm?
7. What would a sustainable week look like for me?
8. What beliefs do I hold about worth and productivity?
9. What kind of work would I choose if income were guaranteed?
10. What small step could move me closer to optional work this month?

Closing Reflection

A life where work is optional is not a fantasy reserved for the privileged—it is a structure that can be built intentionally over time.

It begins with clarity, grows through alignment, and stabilizes through systems that respect your humanity. When work becomes a choice instead of a necessity, creativity replaces survival, and intention replaces pressure.

You do not need to escape your life to reclaim it.

You need to design it—one decision, one system, and one act of self-trust at a time.

Chapter 5: Practical Steps to Financial Independence Now

From Philosophy to Action

Understanding financial independence is powerful—but understanding alone does not change your life. Insight must be translated into structure, and vision must be anchored in action. This chapter is where reflection becomes movement.

Financial independence is not achieved through one dramatic leap. It is built through a series of practical, repeatable decisions that compound over time. The goal is not perfection or instant freedom, but momentum—steady, intentional progress that reshapes your relationship with money and work.

This chapter focuses on *what you can do now*, regardless of income level, background, or circumstance. Financial independence is not reserved for the privileged few. It is built by those willing to observe, adjust, and persist.

Stabilize Before You Scale

Before chasing growth, stability must come first. Many people attempt to build wealth while standing on unstable ground—irregular income, unmanaged expenses, emotional spending, or chronic financial anxiety.

Stability begins with awareness. You must know where your money goes before you can direct it. This doesn't require perfection or complex spreadsheets; it requires honesty.

Stabilization also means creating buffers. Emergency funds, even modest ones, reduce fear-based decision-making. When your survival is not constantly at stake, you can think strategically instead of reactively.

Stability is not stagnation. It is the foundation that allows movement without collapse.

Designing Your Minimum Viable Lifestyle

Financial independence does not start with abundance—it starts with clarity. The concept of a "minimum viable lifestyle" refers to the lowest-cost version of life that still feels dignified, safe, and sustainable for you.

This is not about deprivation. It is about discernment. What do you truly need to function well? What expenses add real value, and which merely fill emotional gaps?

When you understand your baseline, everything changes. You gain leverage. You know exactly what level of income is required to maintain stability, which reduces pressure and opens creative options.

A clear baseline transforms financial goals from abstract dreams into achievable targets.

Building Income That Compounds

Once stability exists, the focus shifts to compounding income. This does not mean working more hours—it means creating systems that grow with time.

Compounding income often comes from digital assets, repeatable services, or scalable skills. The key is that effort today continues to generate value tomorrow.

This approach rewards consistency over intensity. Small, strategic actions repeated regularly outperform sporadic bursts of unsustainable effort.

Think in terms of systems, not hustles. A system works even when motivation dips.

Reducing Dependence, Increasing Choice

Financial independence is less about accumulating wealth and more about reducing dependence. Every bill you eliminate, every skill you learn, and every system you build increases your freedom.

Reducing dependence might mean lowering fixed expenses, diversifying income sources, or building skills that are transferable across industries.

The goal is resilience. When one income stream falters, others remain. When circumstances change, you adapt without panic.

Choice emerges naturally when dependence shrinks.

Consistency Over Intensity

Many people burn out chasing rapid transformation. True independence comes from consistency—small actions repeated long enough to matter.

Consistency builds trust with yourself. It creates momentum. It compounds quietly until progress becomes undeniable.

You don't need to overhaul your life overnight. You need to move in the right direction regularly.

Small steps, taken seriously, reshape your future.

Mindset Shift 1: From Waiting to Building

Waiting assumes permission is required. Building assumes agency.

This shift moves you from passive hope to active creation. You stop waiting for ideal conditions and start using what you have now.

Progress favors those who begin imperfectly.

Mindset Shift 2: From Fear to Experimentation

Fear freezes. Experimentation explores.

When you treat financial moves as experiments rather than final decisions, fear loosens its grip. You test, learn, adjust.

This mindset replaces paralysis with curiosity.

Mindset Shift 3: From Short-Term Relief to Long-Term Freedom

Short-term relief solves today's discomfort. Long-term freedom solves tomorrow's problems.

This shift helps you prioritize actions that build durability rather than temporary comfort.

Freedom is built slowly—but it lasts.

Journal Prompts

1. What does financial independence realistically look like for my current life stage?
2. Which expenses could I reduce without lowering my quality of life?
3. What small income stream could I begin building this month?
4. Where am I relying on hope instead of strategy?
5. What systems could replace my reliance on motivation?
6. How do I respond emotionally to financial uncertainty?
7. What does "enough" look like for me?
8. Where am I resisting simplicity?
9. What daily habit could move me closer to stability?
10. What would change if I trusted myself to adapt?

Closing Reflection

Financial independence is not a finish line—it is a practice. It grows through intention, patience, and the willingness to learn from experience.

You do not need perfect conditions to begin. You need clarity, consistency, and compassion for yourself as you learn.

Each step you take toward stability builds confidence. Each system you create reduces fear. Over time, the life you once imagined becomes the life you inhabit.

This is not about escaping responsibility.

It is about choosing ownership.

And with that choice, your future begins to open.

Appendix A: 12-Month Early Retirement Plan

This appendix translates the philosophy of *The New Rich* into a grounded, realistic, and repeatable 12-month framework. It is not a promise of instant freedom, nor a rigid formula. It is a **strategic map** designed to help you move from financial pressure toward optional work, increased autonomy, and long-term sustainability.

This plan assumes you are starting where you are—without ideal conditions, perfect savings, or unlimited time. It focuses on **stability first, leverage second, freedom last**.

Each month builds on the previous one. Skipping steps weakens the structure. Progress compounds when the foundation is solid.

MONTH 1: Stabilization & Awareness

Primary Goal: Gain clarity and stop financial leakage.

This month is about observation, not optimization. You are building awareness of your current reality without judgment.

Key Actions:

- Track all income and expenses for 30 days.
- Identify fixed vs. variable expenses.
- List financial obligations and deadlines.
- Establish a "financial snapshot" (what comes in, what goes out, what's left).

Mindset Focus:

You are not failing—you are gathering data. Awareness creates control.

Outcome:

A clear understanding of your financial baseline and pressure points.

MONTH 2: Expense Reduction & Financial Breathing Room

Primary Goal: Reduce financial pressure without sacrificing dignity.

This month focuses on removing what drains energy rather than what brings value.

Key Actions:

- Identify 3–5 expenses that can be reduced or eliminated.
- Negotiate bills where possible.
- Simplify subscriptions and recurring costs.
- Begin separating needs from conveniences.

Mindset Focus:
Reduction is not deprivation—it is strategic relief.

Outcome:
Lower monthly obligations and increased psychological space.

MONTH 3: Defining Your Minimum Viable Lifestyle

Primary Goal: Determine what "enough" truly looks like.

This month creates the foundation for optional work by defining your sustainable baseline.

Key Actions:

- Calculate your minimum monthly cost of living with dignity.
- Identify non-negotiables (health, housing, stability).
- Define what "comfort" actually means to you.

Mindset Focus:
Clarity replaces anxiety.

Outcome:
A concrete number representing your personal stability threshold.

MONTH 4: Skill Inventory & Asset Identification

Primary Goal: Identify what you already have that can create value. You are not starting from zero—you are starting from experience.

Key Actions:

- List skills, experiences, and knowledge others might find useful.
- Identify patterns in what people already ask you for.
- Note interests that sustain your energy.

Mindset Focus:
You are more resourced than you think.

Outcome:
A shortlist of viable value offerings.

MONTH 5: Select One Income Stream to Build

Primary Goal: Focus and commitment.

Rather than chasing multiple ideas, you select one direction to develop.

Key Actions:

- Choose one income stream aligned with your skills and energy.
- Define its simplest version (MVP).
- Set realistic expectations for growth.

Mindset Focus:
Progress beats perfection.

Outcome:
A clear, focused income project.

MONTH 6: Build the First Version

Primary Goal: Create the asset, not the masterpiece.
This month is about execution—not polish.

Key Actions:

- Build the first version of your product, service, or system.
- Launch imperfectly.
- Collect feedback rather than validation.

Mindset Focus:
Momentum matters more than mastery.

Outcome:
A functioning asset in the world.

MONTH 7: Optimize and Stabilize

Primary Goal: Improve what exists rather than starting over.

Key Actions:

- Identify what works and what doesn't.
- Simplify delivery and reduce friction.
- Adjust pricing or structure if needed.

Mindset Focus:
Refinement beats reinvention.

Outcome:
A more efficient, sustainable system.

MONTH 8: Automation & Time Recovery

Primary Goal: Reduce manual effort.

Key Actions:

- Automate repetitive tasks.
- Create templates and workflows.
- Streamline customer or client interactions.

Mindset Focus:
Your time is valuable—protect it.

Outcome:
More freedom without loss of output.

MONTH 9: Income Stabilization

Primary Goal: Create predictability.

Key Actions:

- Strengthen recurring revenue if possible.
- Diversify slightly without diluting focus.
- Reinforce systems that generate consistent returns.

Mindset Focus:
Stability enables peace.

Outcome:
Reduced financial volatility.

MONTH 10: Lifestyle Alignment

Primary Goal: Align life design with income reality.

Key Actions:

- Adjust schedule to reflect new freedom.
- Remove obligations that no longer serve you.
- Reinforce routines that support energy and health.

Mindset Focus:
Your life should support your work—not the other way around.

Outcome:
A rhythm that feels sustainable and intentional.

MONTH 11: Reinforcement & Resilience

Primary Goal: Prepare for uncertainty.

Key Actions:

- Build buffers (financial, emotional, logistical).
- Identify potential risks and mitigation strategies.
- Strengthen adaptability.

Mindset Focus:
Resilience is wealth.

Outcome:
Confidence in your ability to weather change.

MONTH 12: Integration & Future Vision

Primary Goal: Solidify independence and plan forward.

Key Actions:

- Review progress and lessons learned.
- Define next-level goals.
- Decide how work fits into your life going forward.

Mindset Focus:
You are no longer chasing freedom—you are practicing it.

Outcome:
A sustainable, self-directed life structure.

Closing Reflection

Early retirement is not a moment—it is a process of alignment. Each month builds upon the last, not through pressure but through clarity and intention.

This plan does not promise ease. It offers direction.

When you focus on stability first, systems second, and freedom third, independence becomes a byproduct rather than a burden.

You are not racing anyone.

You are building a life that supports you—now and into the future.

Message from the Author:

I hope you enjoyed this book, I love astrology and knew there was not a book such as this out on the shelf. I love metaphysical items as well. Please check out my other books:

-Life of Government Benefits

-My life of Hell

-My life with Hydrocephalus

-Red Sky

-World Domination:Woman's rule

-World Domination:Woman's Rule 2: The War

-Life and Banishment of Apophis: book 1

-The Kidney Friendly Diet

-The Ultimate Hemp Cookbook

-Creating a Dispensary(legally)

-Cleanliness throughout life: the importance of showering from childhood to adulthood.

-Strong Roots: The Risks of Overcoddling children

-Hemp Horoscopes: Cosmic Insights and Earthly Healing

- Celestial Hemp Navigating the Zodiac: Through the Green Cosmos

-Astrological Hemp: Aligning The Stars with Earth's Ancient Herb

-The Astrological Guide to Hemp: Stars, Signs, and Sacred Leaves

-Green Growth: Innovative Marketing Strategies for your Hemp Products and Dispensary

-Cosmic Cannabis

-Astrological Munchies

-Henry The Hemp

-Zodiacal Roots: The Astrological Soul Of Hemp

- **Green Constellations: Intersection of Hemp and Zodiac**

-Hemp in The Houses: An astrological Adventure Through The Cannabis Galaxy

-Galactic Ganja Guide
Heavenly Hemp
Zodiac Leaves
Doctor Who Astrology
Cannastrology
Stellar Satvias and Cosmic Indicas
Celestial Cannabis: A Zodiac Journey
AstroHerbology: The Sky and The Soil: Volume 1
AstroHerbology:Celestial Cannabis:Volume 2
Cosmic Cannabis Cultivation
The Starry Guide to Herbal Harmony: Volume 1
The Starry Guide to Herbal Harmony: Cannabis Universe: Volume 2
Yugioh Astrology: Astrological Guide to Deck, Duels and more
Nightmare Mansion: Echoes of The Abyss
Nightmare Mansion 2: Legacy of Shadows
Nightmare Mansion 3: Shadows of the Forgotten
Nightmare Mansion 4: Echoes of the Damned
The Life and Banishment of Apophis: Book 2
Nightmare Mansion: Halls of Despair
Healing with Herb: Cannabis and Hydrocephalus
Planetary Pot: Aligning with Astrological Herbs: Volume 1
Fast Track to Freedom: 30 Days to Financial Independence Using AI, Assets, and Agile Hustles
Cosmic Hemp Pathways
How to Become Financially Free in 30 Days: 10,000 Paths to Prosperity
Zodiacal Herbage: Astrological Insights: Volume 1
Nightmare Mansion: Whispers in the Walls
The Daleks Invade Atlantis
Henry the hemp and Hydrocephalus

10X The Kidney Friendly Diet

Cannabis Universe: Adult coloring book

Hemp Astrology: The Healing Power of the Stars

Zodiacal Herbage: Astrological Insights: Cannabis Universe: Volume 2

Planetary Pot: Aligning with Astrological Herbs: Cannabis Universes: Volume 2

Doctor Who: Convergence Protocol – The Replicator War

Nightmare Mansion: Curse of the Blood Moon

The Celestial Stoner: A Guide to the Zodiac

Cosmic Pleasures: Sex Toy Astrology for Every Sign

Hydrocephalus Astrology: Navigating the Stars and Healing Waters

Lapis and the Mischievous Chocolate Bar

Celestial Positions: Sexual Astrology for Every Sign

Apophis's Shadow Work Journal: **:** A Journey of Self-Discovery and Healing

Kinky Cosmos: Sexual Kink Astrology for Every Sign

Digital Cosmos: The Astrological Digimon Compendium

Stellar Seeds: The Cosmic Guide to Growing with Astrology

Apophis's Daily Gratitude Journal

Cat Astrology: Feline Mysteries of the Cosmos

The Cosmic Kama Sutra: An Astrological Guide to Sexual Positions

Unleash Your Potential: A Guided Journal Powered by AI Insights

Whispers of the Enchanted Grove

Cosmic Pleasures: An Astrological Guide to Sexual Kinks

369, 12 Manifestation Journal

Whisper of the nocturne journal(blank journal for writing or drawing)

The Boogey Book

Locked In Reflection: A Chastity Journey Through Locktober

Generating Wealth Quickly:How to Generate $100,000 in 24 Hours

Star Magic: Harness the Power of the Universe

The Flatulence Chronicles: A Fart Journal for Self-Discovery

The Doctor and The Death Moth

Seize the Day: A Personal Seizure Tracking Journal

The Ultimate Boogeyman Safari: A Journey into the Boogie World and Beyond

Whispers of Samhain: 1,000 Spells of Love, Luck, and Lunar Magic: Samhain Spell Book

Apophis's guides:Witch's Spellbook Crafting Guide for Halloween

Frost & Flame: The Enchanted Yule Grimoire of 1000 Winter Spells

The Ultimate Boogey Goo Guide & Spooky Activities for Halloween Fun

Harmony of the Scales: A Libra's Spellcraft for Balance and Beauty

The Enchanted Advent: 36 Days of Christmas Wonders

Nightmare Mansion: The Labyrinth of Screams

Harvest of Enchantment: 1,000 Spells of Gratitude, Love, and Fortune for Thanksgiving

The Boogey Chronicles: A Journal of Nightly Encounters and Shadowy Secrets

The 12 Days of Financial Freedom: A Step-by-Step Christmas Countdown to Transform Your Finances

Sigil of the Eternal Spiral Blank Journal

A Christmas Feast: Timeless Recipes for Every Meal

Holiday Stress-Free Solutions: A Survival Guide to Thriving During the Festive Season

Yu-Gi-Oh! Holiday Gifting Mastery: The Ultimate Guide for Fans and Newcomers Alike

Holiday Harmony: A Hydrocephalus Survival Guide for the Festive Season

Celestial Craft: The Witch's Almanac for 2025 – A Cosmic Guide to Manifestations, Moons, and Mystical Events

Doctor Who: The Toymaker's Winter Wonderland

Tulsa King Unveiled: A Thrilling Guide to Stallone's Mafia Masterpiece

Pendulum Craft: A Complete Guide to Crafting and Using Personalized Divination Tools

Nightmare Mansion: Santa's Eternal Eve

Starlight Noel: A Cosmic Journey through Christmas Mysteries

The Dark Architect: Unlocking the Blueprint of Existence

Surviving the Embrace: The Ultimate Guide to Encounters with The Hugging Molly

The Enchanted Codex: Secrets of the Craft for Witches, Wiccans, and Pagans

Harvest of Gratitude: A Complete Thanksgiving Guide

Yuletide Essentials: A Complete Guide to an Authentic and Magical Christmas

Celestial Smokes: A Cosmic Guide to Cigars and Astrology

Living in Balance: A Comprehensive Survival Guide to Thriving with Diabetes Insipidus

Cosmic Symbiosis: The Venom Zodiac Chronicles

The Cursed Paw of Ambition

Cosmic Symbiosis: The Astrological Venom Journal

Celestial Wonders Unfold: A Stargazer's Guide to the Cosmos (2024-2029)

The Ultimate Black Friday Prepper's Guide: Mastering Shopping Strategies and Savings

Cosmic Sales: The Astrological Guide to Black Friday Shopping

Legends of the Corn Mother and Other Harvest Myths

Whispers of the Harvest: The Corn Mother's Journal

The Evergreen Spellbook

The Doctor Meets the Boogeyman

The White Witch of Rose Hall's SpellBook

The Gingerbread Golem's Shadow: A Study in Sweet Darkness

The Gingerbread Golem Codex: An Academic Exploration of Sweet Myths

The Gingerbread Golem Grimoire: Sweet Magicks and Spells for the Festive Witch

The Curse of the Gingerbread Golem

10-minute Christmas Crafts for kids

Christmas Crisis Solutions: The Ultimate Last-Minute Survival Guide

Gingerbread Golem Recipes: Holiday Treats with a Magical Twist

The Infinite Key: Unlocking Mystical Secrets of the Ages

Enchanted Yule: A Wiccan and Pagan Guide to a Magical and Memorable Season

Dinosaurs of Power: Unlocking Ancient Magick

Astro-Dinos: The Cosmic Guide to Prehistoric Wisdom

Gallifrey's Yule Logs: A Festive Doctor Who Cookbook

The Dino Grimoire: Secrets of Prehistoric Magick

The Gift They Never Knew They Needed

The Gingerbread Golem's Culinary Alchemy: Enchanting Recipes for a Sweetly Dark Feast

A Time Lord Christmas: Holiday Adventures with the Doctor

Krampusproofing Your Home: Defensive Strategies for Yule

Silent Frights: A Collection of Christmas Creepypastas to Chill Your Bones

Santa Raptor's Jolly Carnage: A Dino-Claus Christmas Tale

Prehistoric Palettes: A Dino Wicca Coloring Journey

The Christmas Wishkeeper Chronicles

The Starlight Sleigh: A Holiday Journey

Elf Secrets: The True Magic of the North Pole

Candy Cane Conjurations

Cooking with Kids: Recipes Under 20 Minutes

Doctor Who: The TARDIS Confiscation

The Anxiety First Aid Kit: Quick Tools to Calm Your Mind

Frosty Whispers: A Winter's Tale

The Infinite Key: Unlocking the Secrets to Prosperity, Resilience, and Purpose

The Grasping Void: Why You'll Regret This Purchase

Astrology for Busy Bees: Star Signs Simplified

The Instant Focus Formula: Cut Through the Noise

The Secret Language of Colors: Unlocking the Emotional Codes

Sacred Fossil Chronicles: Blank Journal

The Christmas Cottage Miracle

Feeding Frenzy: Graboid-Inspired Recipes

Manifest in Minutes: The Quick Law of Attraction Guide

The Symbiote Chronicles: Doctor Who's Venomous Journey

Think Tiny, Grow Big: The Minimalist Mindset

The Energy Key: Unlocking Limitless Motivation

New Year, New Magic: Manifesting Your Best Year Yet

Unstoppable You: Mastering Confidence in Minutes

Infinite Energy: The Secret to Never Feeling Drained

Lightning Focus: Mastering the Art of Productivity in a Distracted World

Saturnalia Manifestation Magick: A Guide to Unlocking Abundance During the Solstice

Graboids and Garland: The Ultimate Tremors-Themed Christmas Guide

12 Nights of Holiday Magic

The Power of Pause: 60-Second Mindfulness Practices

The Quick Reset: How to Reclaim Your Life After Burnout

The Shadow Eater: A Tale of Despair and Survival

The Micro-Mastery Method: Transform Your Skills in Just Minutes a Day

Reclaiming Time: How to Live More by Doing Less
Chronovore: The Eternal Nexus
The Mind Reset: Unlocking Your Inner Peace in a Chaotic World
Confidence Code: Building Unshakable Self-Belief
Baby the Vampire Terrier
Baby the Vampire Terrier's Christmas Adventure
Celestial Streams: The Content Creator's Astrology Manual
The Wealth Whisperer: Unlocking Abundance with Everyday Actions
The Energy Equation: Maximize Your Output Without Burning Out
The Happiness Algorithm: Science-Backed Steps to Joyful Living
Stress-Free Success: Achieving Goals Without Anxiety
Mindful Wealth: The New Blueprint for Financial Freedom
The Festive Flavors of New Year: A Culinary Celebration
The Master's Gambit: Keys of Eternal Power
Shadowed Secrets: Groundhog Day Mysteries
Beneath the Burrow: Lessons from the Groundhog
Spring's Whispers: The Groundhog's Prediction
The Limitless Mindset: Unlock Your Untapped Potential
The Focus Funnel: How to Cut Through Chaos and Get Results
Bold Moves: Building Courage to Live on Your Terms
The Daily Shift: Simple Practices for Lasting Transformation
The Quarter-Life Reset: Thriving in Your 20s and 30s
The Art of Shadowplay: Building Your Own Personal Myth
The Eternal Loop: Finding Purpose in Repetition
Burrowing Wisdom: Life Lessons from the Groundhog
Shadow Work: A Groundhog Day Perspective
Love in Bloom: 5-Minute Romantic Gestures
The Shadowspell Codex: Secrets of Forbidden Magick
The Burnout Cure: Finding Balance in a Busy World
The Groundhog Prophecy: Unlocking Seasonal Secrets
Nog Tales: The Spirited History of Eggnog

Six More Weeks: Embracing Seasonal Transitions
The Lumivian Chronicles: Fragments of the Fifth Dimension
Money on Your Mind: A Beginner's Guide to Wealth
The Focus Fix: Breaking Through Distraction
January's Spirit Keepers: Mystical Protectors of the Cold
Creativity Unchained: Unlocking Your Wildest Ideas in 2025
Manifestation Mastery: 365 Days to Rewrite Your Reality
The Groundhog's Mirror: Reflecting on Change
The Weeping Angels' Christmas Curse
Burrowed in Time: A Groundhog Day Journey
Heartbeats: Poems to Share with Your Valentine
Dino Wicca: The Sacred Grimoire of Prehistoric Magick
Courage of the Pride: Finding Your Inner Roar
The Lion's Leap: Bold Moves for Big Results
Healthy Hustle: Achieving Without Overworking
Practical Manifesting: Turning Dreams into Reality in 2025
Jurassic Pharaohs: Unlocking the Magick of Ancient Egypt and Dino Wicca
The Happiness Equation: Small Changes for Big Joy
The Confidence Compass: Finding Your Inner Strength
Whispers in the Hollow: Tales of the Forgotten Beasts
Echoes from the Hollow: The Return of Forgotten Beasts
The Hollow Ascendant: The Rise of the Forgotten Beasts
The Relationship Reset: Building Better Connections
Mastering the Morning: How to Win the Day Before 8 AM
The Shadow's Dance: Groundhog Day Symbolism
Cupid's Kitchen: Quick Valentine's Day Recipes
Valentine's Day on a Budget: Love Without Breaking the Bank
Astrocraft: Aligning the Stars in the World of Minecraft
Forecasting Life: Groundhog Day Reflections
Bleeding Hearts: Twisted Tales of Valentine's Terror
Herbal Smoke Revolution: The Ultimate Guide to Nature's Cigarette Alternative

Winter's Wrath: The Complete Survival Blueprint for Extreme Freezes.

The Groundhog's Shadow: A Tale of Seasons

Burrowed Insights: Wisdom from the Groundhog

Sensual Strings: The Art of Erotic Bondage

Whispered Flames: Unlocking the Power of Fire Play

Forgotten Shadows: A Guide to Cryptids Lost to Time

Six Weeks of Secrets: Groundhog Day's Hidden Messages

Shadows and Cycles: Groundhog Day Reflections

The Art of Love Letters: Crafting the Perfect Message

Romantic Getaways at Home: Turning Your Space into Paradise

Purrfect Brews: A Cat Lover's Guide to Coffee and Companionship

The Groundhog's Wisdom: Timeless Lessons for Modern Life

The Shadow Oracle: Groundhog Day as a Predictor

Emerging from the Burrow: A Journey of Renewal

The Language of Love: Learning Your Partner's Love Style

Authorpreneur: The Ultimate Blueprint for Writing, Publishing, and Thriving as an Author

Weathering the Seasons: Groundhog Day Perspectives

Valentine's Day Magic: A Guide to Romantic Rituals

The Shadow Chronicles: Stories of Groundhog Day

Love and Laughter: Fun Games for Valentine's Day

AstroRealty: Unlocking the Stars for Property Success

The Groundhog's Path: A Guide to Seasonal Balance

Groundhog Day Diaries: Reflections in the Shadow

The Groundhog's Light: Illuminating the Path Ahead

Valentine's Traditions from Around the World

AI Wealth Revolution: Unlocking the Trillionaire Mindset

Love Rekindled: Reigniting Passion in Relationships

Single and Thriving: Self-Love on Valentine's Day

Emerald Legends: Mystical Tales of Ireland

Green Alchemy: Harnessing Nature's Magic
The Hearts of Horror: A Valentine's Day Nightmare
The Leprechaun's Guide to Wealth and Wisdom
Dancing with the Sidhe: Celebrating the Otherworld
Shamrocks and Shadows: Mysteries of the Green Isle
Emerald Energy: Harnessing Luck and Growth
The Gingerbread Golem's Valentine: A Sweetheart's Guide to Love and Enchantment
The Celtic Knot: Weaving Life and Destiny
Green Fire: Elemental Magic for St. Patrick's Day
Clover Chronicles: Finding Your Inner Luck
Ireland's Mystical Creatures: A Field Guide
Gingerbread Golem's Love Almanac
Prowl and Thrive: The Lion's Guide to Success
Love Alchemy: Transforming Your Life Through Heart Energy
WORLD DOMINATION: Woman's Rule 3:The New Life
The Midnight Rose: A Guide to Lunar Love Spells
The Forbidden Letters: Writing Your Own Love Prophecy
Luck and Lore: St. Patrick's Day for Modern Mystics
The Green Path: A Pagan Celebration of Renewal
The Dark Architect's Guide to Reprogramming Reality
Prankster's Paradise: A Guide to Harmless Hijinks
Manifest Your Reality: The Law of Attraction Simplified
The TARDIS Owner's Manual: Understanding the Doctor's Ship: *A complete guide to the TARDIS, its technology, secrets, and mysteries*
Starlit Romance: Astrology Secrets for Finding True Love
The Time Lord's Atlas: A Complete Guide to the Whoniverse: ***A breakdown of the locations, planets, and dimensions explored in Doctor Who***
Sweetheart Shadows: The Dark Side of Love and Attraction
February Fire: Reigniting Passion in Every Area of Life

The Self-Love Toolkit: 5 Ways to Embrace Who You Are
February Sparks: Ignite Your Dreams in 28 Days
March to Success: A 31-Day Action Blueprint
Ancient Paths: The 13 Sacred Principles of Dino Wicca
Echoes of Tomorrow: Navigating the AI Revolution
The Wellness Blueprint: Balancing Mind, Body, and Soul
Green Horizons: Sustainable Living for a Better Tomorrow
The AI Wealth Code: How to Make Millions with Automation
AI-Powered Creativity: Writing, Art, and Music for Profit
Extinction Rites: Rebirthing Your Soul Through Prehistoric Magick
Sacred Serpents tarot
Celestial Enchantment blank journal
Star Strains
Culinary Journeys: Exploring Global Flavors at Home
The Hollowvale Curse
The Hollowvale Harvest
The Egg of Transformation: Awakening Your Inner Power
Blooming Into Power: A Wiccan Guide to Spring Awakening
The Nightmare Nexus: The Third Doctor's Perilous Haunting
Digital Detox: Reclaiming Your Life in a Connected World
Ostara's Path: Walking the Spiral of Renewal
The Sacred Hare
Financial Freedom: Building Wealth in the Modern Age
Spring's Cauldron: Stirring the Waters of Change
The Hollowvale Pact
Quantum Consciousness: The Science of Reality Shifting
The Hollowvale Hunger
The Sacred Waters Within: A Witch's Guide to Hydrocephalus Magick
The Raven's Nest: Building a Life of Unshakable Stability
AI and the Human Mind: The Future of Intelligence
The Hollowvale Reckoning

Timeless Love: Building and Maintaining Lasting Relationships

The Raven's Roar: Unlocking Unstoppable Confidence

Raven Sight: Awakening Intuition and Inner Wisdom

The Butterfly Effect: Small Changes, Big Transformations

Taming the Boogeyman: How to Conquer Your Inner Fears

The Magick of Green: Awakening Earth's Energy in You

The Entrepreneurial Mindset: Secrets to Business Success

The Hollowvale End

The Shadow Luck Ritual: Reclaiming Power from Your Dark Side

Spring Magick for Beginners: A Simple Guide to Seasonal Energy Work

Doctor Who: The Hollowvale Conundrum

The March of Miracles: Unlocking Synchronicities in Spring

Unveiling the Cosmos: A Guide to Stargazing and Space Exploration

The Ultimate Guide to Surviving an Economic Collapse

The AI Gold Rush: How to Profit from the AI Revolution

Bastet's Shadow: The Hidden Power of Feline Magick

The Bastet Codex: Unlocking the Goddess's Magickal Secrets

Purring Spells: Harnessing Bastet's Healing Frequencies

Bastet's Nine Lives: Rebirth, Transformation, and Immortality Spells

Primal Currents: Hydrocephalus Magick in the Path of Dino Wicca

The Digital Gold Rush: Mastering E-Commerce and Online Sales

Future Shock: Adapting to the Next Decade of Change

The Quantum Mindset: Think Like a Billionaire

Sacred Motherhood: Awakening the Divine Feminine Within

The Mother's Spellbook: Enchantments for Love, Protection, and Prosperity

The Witch's Guide to Parenting: Raising Empowered and Intuitive Children
The Magick of Motherhood: Reclaiming Your Power Through Rituals
The Pagan Path to Self-Love: A Goddess's Guide to Worth and Confidence
Wild Woman Magick: Unleashing Your Primal Power
The Money Magnet Blueprint: Unlocking Unlimited Wealth
Biohacking 101: Unlock Your Body's Full Potential
The Wild Father: A Pagan Guide to Strength and Wisdom
The Sacred Masculine: Unlocking Your Inner Power
The Druid's Compass
The Warrior's Mindset
The Father's Fire
Odin's Path
Ancestral Bonds
The House That Whispers
The Magician's Code
The Wild Hunt
The Green Man's Path
The Altar of Success
The Shadow and the Sword
The High Priestess's Guide to Energy Healing
The Lunar Mother
The Sacred Self-Care Grimoire
The Womb Wisdom Codex
The Wheel of the Mother
The Witch's Guide to Manifestation
The Q2 Reset
The Ultimate Guide to AI-Powered Passive Income
Escape the 9-5
AI Feline Fortunes
The Tear-Stained Grimoire

Razorblade Runes
Cemetery Sirens
The Midnight Wristwatch
The Town That Forgets
AI Horror & Creepypasta
The Hollow Frequency
The Breach Echo
The Quiet Between Worlds
The Sigil of Tharan-Khul
Summon the Vault of Y'ha'ten
The Becoming Codex
The Profit of Az'ra-nar
The Drowned Logos
Echoes of the Eldritch Will
The Deep Ledger
Necronomicon of Networth
Covenant of the Wealthwyrm
The Whisperer's Manifesto
The Rites of Azh-K'luth
The Ark of the Crawling Coin
The Tithe of Shadows
Inkheart Abyss
The Timewinds of Y'ha-nthlei
The Spiral Labyrinth of Azag-Nirrh
The Gallifreyan Heresy of the Black Pharaoh
The Psalms of Nyog-Sotha
Black Rain Alchemy
The Infinite Maw
The Entropic Blueprint
The Oracle of Sh'guul
The Book of Breach
The Drowned Saint's Testament
Dreamcraft of the Sleeper God

The Silence Market
Cthonomics: The Dark Wealth Algorithm
Invocation of the Ten-Eyed King
Wealthbound to the Wyrm Below
Become the Unnameable
Codex of the Sovereign Flame
Rituals of Relentless Becoming
The Shadow Ascends
The Eyes Beneath You
The Will That Wakes Worlds
Silence Is a Weapon
The Mirror That Screams
The Whisper Between Moments
The Mind That Devours Fear
The Myth of the Finished Self
The Architect of Your Madness
The Voice You've Buried
The Discipline of Madness
Stormborn: Awakening Your Inner Tempest
The Mind That Ate Time
Unbind Your Becoming
The Pact You Owe Yourself
The Devourer's Diet
The Acid That Carves the Path
The Tower You Must Burn
The Breath Between Worlds
Speak Like the Deep
The Labyrinth Within
The Spine of the Sea God
Rejection Is a Portal
The Crown You Refused
The Scar Is the Spell
The Lightless Flame

The Habit of Becoming Horrific
ChickenJockey Chaos
The Gatekeeper Within
You Are Not Your Name
The Compass of the Mad
The Archive of Unsent Letters
What the Mirror Can't Show You
The Knife You Needed
Worship Nothing, Become Everything
The Other Voice
The Body the World Forgot
The Vein of the Void
The Black Bone Codex
The Puzzle of the Hidden Self (Millennium Puzzle)
The Eye That Sees the Lie *(Millennium Eye)*
The Ring of Return (Millennium Ring)
The Rod of Relentless Will ***(Millennium Rod)***
The Tally of the Soul (Millennium Tauk/Necklace)
The Key to the Locked Timeline (Millennium Key)
The Scale of Sacred Decisions (Millennium Scales)
Inferno Bites: The UnOfficial Minecraft Lava Cookbook
Rot in the Attic
Prana: The Hidden Force of Your Infinite Self
The Shadow Realm Within: Transforming Darkness Into Destiny
The Borderland Collapse
Claws of Protection: Bastet's Defensive Magick
Mr. Ring-a-Ding's Madness
Yugioh Astrology: Celestial Deckcraft and Duel Destiny (2026–2027 Edition)
The Seal You Signed: Unlocking the Power You Once Feared
The Puzzle of Infinite Minds: Unlocking the Mentalism Hidden Within

The Eye That Mirrors the All: Secrets of Inner Reflection
Doctor Who: The Toymaker's Broadcast
The Rod of Eternal Flow: Commanding the Currents of Vibration
Golden Eyes of Bastet: Enhancing Psychic Vision
The Key of Dual Forces: Balance Within the Polarity
The Scales of Living Rhythm: Timing the Dance of Life
The Necklace of Hidden Cause: Weaving the Webs of Fate
The Ring of Secret Masters: Rising Through the All Within All
Daggers of the Dying Deep
Bastet's Wealth and Fortune Magick: Prosperity Rituals of the Goddess
The Tide that Speaks
The Scrolls of Petosiris: 13 Rituals from the Feathered Eye
Petosiris and the Living Plague of Osirion
Feline Fire: Bastet's Passion and Love Magick
The Star Altar of Petosiris
Bastet's Whiskers: Supernatural Sensory Magick
The Bastet Grimoire
Feeding the Shadows
The Mouthless Prayer
The Spiral Wound
Becoming the Ibis: Lessons from Petosiris's Mind
The Crimson Coven: Cola Magick for Sweet Dominion
Sacred Cat's Paw
The Soda Zodiac: A Flavor for Every Sign
Covenant of the Crawling Flame
The Ink of Ish'Zur
Frothroot: The Thirst That Ate the World
The Golden Glyphs of Prosperity
The Etherbind Codex
Echoes of the Resistance: Reclaiming the You That Survived

Harnessed Minds: Breaking Free from Mental Control
The Eyes in the Smoke
Rootwake: The Carbon Covenant
Skitter Logic: Unlearning the Fear That Built You
Doctor Who: The World That Froths
Rootwake: The Fizz That Rewrites Flesh
Rootwake: Frothfather of the World
The Holly Pact: Blood Beneath the Mistletoe
The 2nd Mass Principle: Building Unbreakable Tribes
Web of Wits: A Survival Guide to Encounters with Anasi the Spider (Aunt Nancy)
The Hexbreaking Handbook: Effective Spells to Remove Curses
Pop Alchemy: Transform Your Life One Sip at a Time
The Mason Code: Leading in Unleadable Times
Petosiris and the Fifth Chamber of Thoth
The Ether Seed Within
The Parent of Tomorrow
Petosiris's Pyramid of Perpetual Wealth
Unlearn the World
Grimoire of the Hollow Tongue
Zodiac Weeds: Finding Your Strain Through the Stars
Aquarius Rises in the Bank
The Sugar God's Smile
The Skinclock Reversal: Biohacking the Face of Time
Debtburn: How to Obliterate What You Owe Forever
The Ice Cream Oracle: What Your Cone Says About Your Future
Silence Is Sovereignty: The Power of Being Unreadable
The Wind That Whispers Through Stone
Path of the Four Directions
Doctor Who: The Maestro's Symphony of Endings
Oxygen Grail: Breathing to Undo the Clock

Zodiacal Collapse: When Stars Devour Time

Teachings from the Red Sand Silence

Doctor Who: Omega – The Broken Equation

Memory Wipe Your Past: Start Over Like a MiB

Mitochondria Prime: Ignite the Core of Youth

A Nest of Roaches

Grub from the Galaxy: MiB Recipes You'll Never Forget

Whiskers of Power: Bastet's Guide to Inner Sovereignty

The Gift Must Cost Them: Negotiation Through Unequal Exchange

The Worm Guys' Wealth Code: Hustle Like an Alien

Bug Out: The Edgar Method for Ruthless Goal Setting

Weaving Life with Spiderwoman's Pattern

Doctor Who: The Rani's Renaissance

How to Get a Job (If You're a Puppygirl)

Speak Through Others: The Art of Proxy Power

T-Rex Your Trauma: Reclaim the Power of Your Primal Self

The Black Briefcase: How MiB Stay Wealthy in Silence

The Thirst Beyond Reason: Understanding Diabetes Insipidus From the Inside Out

Backwoods Witchcraft for Billionaires: The Pagan Path from Dirt Roads to Gold Roads

The Moonshine Grimoire: Fermented Spells for Abundance

The Nameless Geometry

The Wraith's Mixtape: Spellcasting with Songs of Sorrow

The Gallifreyan Gentleman: Silent Wealth, Sonic Confidence, and the Doctor's Code of Living

Sugar Water Confidence

Dino Totems: Spirit Guides from Earth's First Gods

Pumpkin Sigils & Ritual Smoke

The Hózhó Compass

The Distortus Discipline – Order from Inner Mutation

Witchcraft for the Cold-Blooded Soul

Moonlight Over the Blessingway
Water, Interrupted: When the Body Forgets How to Hold On
Deformed but Divine: Embracing Your Asymmetry
Hexes in the Henhouse: The Farm Witch's Guide to Power
The Reversed Flame: A Grimoire of Inverted Power
Salt, Cells, and Sanity: Reclaiming Balance with Diabetes Insipidus
King of the Broken: Crowning the Flawed Self
Moonlight Scars: Emo Moon Magick and the Art of Lunar Sorrow
Noose Spells: Magick of the Hanging Rope
The Goth Cathedral: Rituals of the Broken and Beautiful
The Cretaceous Codex: Dino Spirits and Fossil Magick
The Turkey Bones Ritual
Nine Lives of Manifestation: Unlocking Bastet's Reality Codes
Chaos Muscles: Building Strength from Twisted Pain
Emo Blood Magick: The Veins of Power
The 3AM Flood: Nighttime Urination, Sleep Loss, and the DI Spiral
The Silence Between the Stars
The Lemon Method: Sour Your Way to Success
Starlit Sovereign
The Rite of Twelve Gates: Walking the Gates of the Duat.
Cornbread and Conjure: Recipes for Riches and Rootwork
The Black Rose Rituals: Emo Love Spells and Obsession Magick
The Eternal Goodbye: Death Magick and Rebirth Rituals
Sinkrot: The Drain That Remembers
The Hybrid Mindset: Thinking Beyond Evolution
Bone Dry: Navigating Dehydration Before It Breaks You
Wreathcraft: Winter Sigils and Yuletide Spells
The Rite of Twelve Mouths

S'mores of the Damned: Haunted Recipes for Halloween Night

Rethink the Drink: A Beverage Survival Guide for DI Warriors

The Shadow Chord: Guitar Magick and Sonic

Malformed Yet Majestic: Leading When You Feel Wrong Inside

The Cursed Diary: Ink-Stained Spells of the Emo Soul

Anxiety Off Switch: Emergency Reset for a Fried Nervous System

The Energy Heist: How to Take Back Your Life from Drainers

Beyond the Bathroom: Rebuilding Your Social Life With DI

Coyote's Gift for Decision Makers

Ghoul-Goo: Spooky S'mores You'll Die For

Echoes in the Mirror: Scrying and Self-Destruction Magick

Thread and Thorn: Stitching Spells from Rural Cloth

The Mogwai Mind: Building Untouchable Wealth from Small Ideas

Be Your Own Guide: Trust Your Inner Compass

Hormones in Chaos: The Endocrine Puzzle of Diabetes Insipidus

ChronoCleanse: Detox Your Biological Timeline

The Limb You Hide Is the One That Saves You

Leaves, Bones, and Whisper Spells

The Dinosaur Mindset: Prehistoric Tactics for Modern Wealth

Clawing Back Control: A Bastet Method for Boundaries and Empowerment

Samhain Codes of the Forgotten

Orange Alchemy: The Autumnal Spellbook

Monster Within, Master Without

The Sigil That Sleeps

Hearthcraft: Yule Hearth Sigils and Winter Warmth Spells

Temple of the Purring Moon: Rituals from Bastet's Lineage
When the Earth Remembers Your Footsteps
Food for Mood: Eat to Heal Depression, Not Just Survive It
Witch of the Kudzu Vine: Southern Pagan Wealth Secrets
The Invisible Diagnosis: Advocating for Yourself With DI
The Coffin's Lullaby: Sleep Magick and Nightmares as Portals
Ashes of the Will: Rituals for Erasing the Self
The Fracture Rite: Shattering the Magickal Core
Funeral Candles: The Art of Emo Flame Magick
The Black Grimoire: A Blank Ritual for Writing in Absence
Phantom Thirst: A Halloween Survival Guide for Diabetes Insipidus
The Hollow Crown: Emo Royalty and Magick of the Outcast King
Sandpainting for the Soul
Falling Into Balance: Using the Extra Hour to Recalibrate Life
100 Southern Superstitions That Still Work
The DI Child: A Parent's Guide to Raising Hydrated, Happy Kids
The Jungle of Shame: Escaping the Hidden Lab of Doubt
The Witch's Toast: S'mores Spells and Creepy Confections
The Hoodoo Pantry: Spells from the Mason Jar
The Immortal Fortune: Secret Wealth Lessons from Captain Jack Harkness
The Specter's Embrace: Magick for Channeling Ghostly Lovers
Grateful Waters: A Thanksgiving Survival Guide for Diabetes Insipidus
The Seizure Gospel
Harvestbind: Autumn Sigils and Samhain Spells
Doctor Who: The Algorithmic Awakening
Silent Nights, Steady Waters: A Christmas Survival Guide for Diabetes Insipidus

The Extra Hour Effect: How One Hour Can Transform Everything

Blade Between the Breaths

Running with the Mountain Shadows

Echoes of the Failed Experiment – Becoming a Living Legacy

Swamp Witches & River Ghosts: Real Southern Hauntings

Cornbread Prophecies: Magical Recipes from a Southern Table

Doctor Who: The Signal in the Star

Bloomcraft: Spring Sigils and Equinox Enchantments

Vanisher: How to Disappear from the Internet Without Losing Your Life

The Ultimate Christmas Cookie Cookbook

The Unbreakable Parent: How to Mentally Survive Raising Kids in a Broken World

Time Debt: How to Reclaim the Hours You Didn't Know You Lost

One Month, One Million: Unconventional Cash Creation Tactics

Doctor Who: The Cyber Conversion Protocol

Black Friday Frenzy: The Art of Finding Hidden Online Deals

The Grimoire Buried Under the Apple Tree

Digital Couponing Masterclass: Your Step-by-Step Guide to Black Friday Savings

The Fire Inside the Flint

Shadows on the Ceiling: The Emo Guide to Astral Magick

The Bone-Eaters Beneath Us

Black Friday Bundle Blueprint: Creating Irresistible Product Packages for Maximum Sales

Thirteen Nights of Unbinding

Doctor Who: Engines of Influence

Pumpkin Spice Alchemy: Recipes of Fire and Frost

When Raptor Met Rexy: Prehistoric Lessons in Wild Romance

Oblivion's Candle: Burn the Path Behind You

Campfire Curses and Chocolate: A Halloween S'mores Grimoire

The Wallet That Wasn't Mine: Breaking Free from Inherited Scarcity

The Cola Zodiac: What Your Fizz Says About Your Fate

Frostfire Fortune: Unlocking Winter's Hidden Prosperity

Signal Jamming: Detox Your Brain from Info Overload

The Dust of the Forgotten Rite

The Golden Cat Sigils: Drawing Power in Bastet's Name

Mud Magick: The Prosperity of Getting Dirty

Savory Spicefall: Beyond the Pumpkin Pie

Pumpkin Spice Apothecary Kitchen

The Pumpkin Spice Economy: Turning Trends into Billions

The Ember Veil: 13 Nights of Fire Magick

Financial Freeze: When Earning Triggers Panic

The Gingerbread Alchemist: Sweet Recipes with a Twist

Biosynth Power: Programming Yourself from Scratch

Echoes from the Talking Circle

Truffle Alchemy: Fungus of Fortune

Spores of Power: The Truffle Witch's Handbook

Doctor Who: The Tower That Speaks

The Mycelium Veil: Truffle Magick Unbound

Broke But Ashamed: Healing the Shame Wound of Debt

The Evergreen Mind: Growth Through Winter Stillness

The Black Veil Truffle Rite

The Voice Beneath Symbols

Witchlight on the Bayou: Swamp Spells for Sovereignty

I Grew Up Poor and Now I Sabotage My Success

The Lantern of Hollow Souls

Shutdown Survival: A Citizen's Guide to Thriving When Government Stops

When Abundance Feels Like a Threat: Healing the Hidden Fears of Enough

The Scarecrow Grimoire

Owls of the October Veil

Candlewax and Curses: A Halloween Spellbook

Excavating the Inner Fossil – Transforming Fossilized Thoughtforms into Tools of Power

The Yule Witch's Spellbook: Magick for the Holiday Season

Haunted Christmas: Ghost Stories for Winter Nights

The Christmas Survival Guide: Thriving Through the Chaos

The Bone Orchard Rites

Haunted Commerce: The Ghost in the Marketplace

When Money Triggers the Inner Child

Silent Night with the Silence: A Christmas Thriller

The Lightning Crown: Living and Leading Through Seizures

TARDIS Tidings: Festive Stories from the Whoniverse

Autumn Reset: Slowing Down Without Falling Behind

The Trillion Dollar Soul: Rewriting the Currency of Reality

Truffle Eclipse Magick

Micro-Manifestations: Quick Magick That Works

5-Minute Rituals for Busy Witches

The Marshmallow Massacre: Halloween Treats with a Sinister Twist

Blood and Blackberry Thorns

Magickal Mornings: Rituals for a Blessed Christmas Day

Embers of the All-Hallows Fire

The Pumpkin Market Collapse

The Hour You Gained: Transforming Time Into Power

The Chamber Must Be Sealed: Mastering the Power of Controlled Access

The Cursed Manuscript of Petosiris

The Festive Hearth: Creating Holiday Traditions
Darkness Rising: Thriving as Nights Grow Longer
Harvesting Time: Turning the Year's End Into Your New Beginning
Petosiris and the 13th Zodiac Key
Wagewound: When Paychecks Become Identity Prisons
Walls That Watch
The Silent Feast: Rituals of Power in the Longest Night
The Distortus Legacy : Becoming a Deformed King in a Perfect World
The Hollow Masks
The Gratitude Furnace: Forging Gold from Thanks
Feast of Inner Gold: Eating for Energy and Enlightenment
Haunted Commerce: The Season of Spending Spirits
Fear Bonds: How Panic Creates Profit
Black Friday E-Commerce Playbook: Sales Tactics to Skyrocket Your Holiday Revenue
Budgeting for Black Friday: A Holiday Savings Planner
Haunting the Harvest Moon
The Warrior's Water: Emergency Preparedness for People With DI
The First Sip of the Year: A New Year's Survival Guide for Diabetes Insipidus
Doctor Who: The Thirteenth Node
The Unseen Struggle: Mental Health, Anxiety, and Chronic Thirst
The Hearth's Hidden Ledger: Counting Energies as Currency
The Gift Alchemist: Turning Any Offering Into Gold
The Papyrus of the Bound Spirit
The Magick of Leftovers: Transmutation in the Fridge
Frost and Fortune: Christmas Wealthcraft for the Modern Magus
Last-Minute Gifts: Creative Ideas on a Budget

10 Secrets to Surviving Holiday Crowds
The Witch's Dow Jones
The Witches' Graveyard Shift
Pumpkin Sigils: Carving Rites for Midnight Power
The Secret Shopper's Black Friday Guide: How to Get Early Access and VIP Deals
Fever in the Foundation
The Neuralyzer Reset: Reprogram Your Morning Routine
Lightning Lessons of the White Painted Woman
The Enchanted Snowflake
The Magic Sip: Surviving Disney Parks with Diabetes Insipidus
The One Who Draws Through You
Santa's Secrets: A Magical Holiday Planner
Silent Bells, Loud Miracles: Self-Help for the Season of Stillness
The Sugar Spell Codex: Confectionary Magick of Christmas
Autumn Hexcraft: Fallen Leaves, Fallen Barriers
Sleep Like a Fortress: Build a Life Where Insomnia Can't Survive
Nowhere Was Ever Home
Christmas Under the Stars: A Celestial Holiday Guide
Rentproof: How to Never Be Evicted Again
Workless: Escape the 9-5 Without Being Broke
The Gilded Gift: A Wealth Altar for Christmas Morning
The Black Friday Grimoire
The Hollowing: Ceremonies of Spiritual Collapse
Doctor Who: The Nameless Signal
Where the Eagle Hides His Courage
The Dwarf Tyrant's Ascent: Claiming Power in a World of Giants
The Currency of the Dead: Trading with Spectral Bankers
The Icebound Witch: Survival and Magick in the Cold

The Emergency Money Mind: Constant Crisis, Zero Calm

Thirst & Roses: A Valentine's Survival Guide for Diabetes Insipidus

Springing Into Clarity: Mastering the Energy Shift of Daylight Saving

Speed of the Nanotyrant: Agile Strategies for Life's Hunt

The 90-Day Reset: A Science-Backed Guide to Reinvent Yourself Before the New Year

The Coil of Thorns

Timegates Unleashed

Dopamine Fasting 2.0: Rewiring Your Brain in a World of Overstimulation

The Nanotyrannus Mutation: Embracing Your Differentiated Form

Unwritten January: How to Use the Blank Page of the Year to Re-Author Your Life

Feast of the Forgotten Spirits: Ancestor Magick for the Holidays

The Burnout Codex: A System for Thriving Beyond Stress

I Don't Deserve to Have Money

When the King Doesn't See You: The Shadow Predator's Guide

The Reset Ritual :A Guide to Shedding Last Year's Weight—Emotional and Physical—by Spring Cleaning Your Soul

Calendar Alchemy: Learn to Bend Time and Productivity around Your Natural Rhythms

The Mirror Contract: A One-Sentence Agreement with Yourself that Unlocks Real Change

The Nile Formula: Sacred Flow for Millionaire Minds

Forward Momentum: Productivity Rituals for the Lost Hour

Harvest Gold: Wealth Magick of Pumpkin Spice Commerce

The Magick of Christmas Lights: Illuminating Holiday Rituals

Cranberry Crown: Royal Self-Worth through Ritual Meals
Petosiris and the Worms of the Feathered Throne
The Evergreen Equation: Self-Help for Sustained Growth
The Rain Will Wash Us Away: Emo Weather Magick
Snowlight Shadows: Magick Under Frozen Stars
Doctor Who: Merger of Empires
The Light Within the Feast: Magickal Wealth of Yuletide Flame
Momentum Machines: Small Habits Designed to Snowball into Unstoppable Forward Motion
Calm Spells: Magickal Solutions for Anxiety Relief
Santa's Final List: The Naughty Never Leave
The Mystic's Guide to Banishing Worry
The Silence Dividend: Turning Quiet Mornings into Compounding Growth All Year
Charmed Stillness: Rituals to Ease the Mind
Blood Spiral Ascension
The Vanishing Heart Invocation
Crystal Calm: Harnessing Stones for Anxiety
The Nano Tyrant Code: Strength in the Small Predator
The Energy Ledger: Accounting Methods for Vitality, Not Just Money
Snowglobe Mindset: Shake Up Your Thoughts, Settle Into Peace
The Weight of the Feather: Anubis's Codes for Soul Balance
Pocket Peppermint Power: Tiny Rituals for Big Holiday Energy
Shadowkeeper of the Golden Jackal: Anubis's Path to Energetic Protection
The Witch's Breath: Anxiety Relief Through Magickal Breathing
The Tiny Ember: Pocket Motivation for Cold Days

The Twelfth Doctor: The Rebel with a Cause (Peter Capaldi, 2013–2017)

The Thirteenth Doctor: Breaking the Mold
(Jodie Whittaker, 2017–2022)

The Fourteenth Doctor: A New Beginning (David Tennant, 2022–2023)

The Fifteenth Doctor: Rewriting the Stars
(Ncuti Gatwa, 2023–2025)

Santa's Shortcut to Success: Micro Habits for a Better New Year

The Midnight Cocoa Manifesto: Comfort Rituals for Hard Nights

Why I Can't Save: Trauma Blocks to Financial Planning

Dino Brain, Mega Goals: Rewire Yourself for Savage Success.

Jurassic Profit: Unearth Your Inner Millionaire Fossil

Scales & Softness: Dating with Dino Heart

Carnotaurus Dreams.

Red Willow Thinking.

Reindeer Resilience: How to Keep Going When You're Exhausted

Candlewick Courage: Lighting Strength in Dark Seasons.

Elf-Mode Focus: Fast Attention Fixes for Busy Seasons

Futureproof Feelings: Emotional Skill-Building for Resilience No Matter What the New Year Brings

The 90-Day Rewire: Transform Your Neural Pathways Before Spring Blooms

Jolly Rich: Christmas Micro-Money Magick for Fast Prosperity.

Gingerbread Gratitude: Mini Practices for a Happier Holiday

Trauma-Spending: When Money Becomes a Drug

Goal Skeletons: Build Minimalist Frameworks for Resolutions That Last

The Snarl Strategy: Growling Back at a World That Silenced You

The Hourglass Reset: Reclaiming What the Clock Took

Yule Claw: Dino Rites of Light in the Darkness

Sacred Circles: Grounding Rituals for Anxious Souls

Clockstopper's Gut: Rebuilding the Core of Time

Winterfire Drive: Harness the Cold Season's Stillness to Ignite Deep Motivation

The 5-Minute Productivity Hack: Small Steps to Big Results

Light Ascending: A Self-Help Guide to Longer Days

Inner Economy: Trade Self-Doubt for Confidence Like a High-Value Currency

Simple Success: Decluttering Your Life for Better Results

The Resilient Mind: Thriving in Tough Times

The 2026 Playbook: Mastering the Year Ahead

The Spring Sleep Solution: Conquering Fatigue After Time Change.

The Hormonal Compass: Navigate Back to Your Youth

Golden Vision: Eating for Your Eye Color with the Power of Ghee

Lionhearted Love: Strength in Relationships

MiB Mindset: Think Like a Cosmic Agent

The Ladder of Small Wins: Climb Out of Stagnation by Stacking Micro-Victories

The Momentum Hour: Gaining More in Less Time.

The Year of You: A Self-Help Blueprint for Unapologetic Self-Ownership

The Dust That Watches You Back.

The Astral Parent

Shadow of the King: The Nanotyrannus Parable

Tiny Tidings of Triumph: Small Wins That Change Your Life

Dwarf Tyrant Rising: When You're the One They Overlook

The Bank Account Mirror: Healing How You See Yourself Through Money

Cretaceous Black

When Love Costs Too Much: Romantic Triggers and Financial Wounds

Dream-Eater's Guide to Wealth

Unzipped Reality: The Jacket That Opens Portals

The Power of No: How to Set Boundaries and Get Rich

Keeper of the Desert Veil: Anubis's Teachings on Illusion & Truth

Redacted Stargates: Stories the SGC Buried

The Clock That Dripped Time

Doctor Who: The Silent Acquisition

Hairline Manifestation: Unlocking Power at the Edge of Thought

Cash-Eater Crickets: How Insects Predict Economic Collapse

Dead Pet Whisperer: Grief Alchemy from the Other Side

The Love Algorithm Is Broken: Hack Romance Before It Hacks You

The Rite of the 8-Limbed Seal

Melt the Moon: A Fire Ritual to Reshape Emotion

Venomous Miracles: Healing Through the Poison Path

Wealth Without Water: The Post-Aquatic Rich Life

The Butterfly Betrayal: When Change Turns on You

The Quiet Upgrade: How Humans Are Secretly Rebuilding Themselves Without Asking Permission

Nobody Taught Us This: The Missing Human Manual for Money, Energy, and Self-Respect

You Were Never Broken: Why Most People Are Reacting Normally to an Unstable World

After the Noise Ends: How Humans Reset When the World Finally Goes Quiet

<u>The Month That Tells the Truth: Why January Reveals What the Rest of the Year Hides</u>

Tremors Party Unleashed: The Ultimate Guide to a Graboids Birthday Bash

Cold Start Human: Rebooting Motivation Without Forcing Momentum

The Year that doesn't start until they say

Love Without Performance: What Connection Looks Like When No One Is Watching

February Is a Mirror: What Love Exposes About You

How We Learned Love Wrong: Uninstalling Cultural Myths About Connection

You Are Not Too Much: Why Needing Love Is Not a Flaw

The Crooked Fence Covenant: Backwoods Boundaries and Witch Wealth

The Day That Keeps Repeating: Why Your Life Feels Stuck—and How to Shift It Gently

Nothing Changes Until Something Softens: Escaping Repetition Without Violence to Yourself

Same Life, Different Ending: How Tiny Choices Rewrite Repetition

The Loop Isn't Punishment: Why You're Being Asked to Learn, Not Suffer

Panic at the Register: Retail Anxiety and Public Shame

The Secret Formula to Becoming an Influencer in 90 Days

Get Some Tarot cards: https://www.makeplayingcards.com/sell/apophis-occult-shop

Get some shirts: https://www.bonfire.com/store/apophis-shirt-emporium/

<u>Instagrams:</u>
@apophis_enterprises,
@apophisbookemporium,
@apophisscardshop
Twitter: @apophisenterpr1 Tiktok:@apophisenterprise
Youtube: @sg1fan23477
Hive: @sg1fan23477
CheeLee: @SG1fan23477

Podcast: Apophis Chat Zone: https://open.spotify.com/show/5zXbrCLEV2xzCp8ybrfHsk?si=fb4d4fdbdce44dec

Newsletter: https://apophiss-newsletter-27c897.beehiiv.com/

If you want to support me or see posts of other projects that I have come over to: **buymeacoffee.com/mpetchinskg**

I post there daily several times a day

www.ingramcontent.com/pod-product-compliance
Lightning Source LLC
LaVergne TN
LVHW022007200926
848481LV00007B/2270
9798295515101